GW00708253

Why Worry?

By Beth Mende Conny

Illustrated by Paula Brinkman

PETER PAUPER PRESS, INC.

WHITE PLAINS, NEW YORK

Designed by Mullen & Katz
Illustrations copyright © 1999
Paula Brinkman

Text copyright © 1999
Peter Pauper Press, Inc.
202 Mamaroneck Avenue
White Plains, NY 10601
ISBN 0-88088-386-3
Printed in China
7 6 5 4 3 2 1

Why Worry?

Worry is flab;
action
is muscle.

Worries are
a part of life,
not a
way of life.

Fill your life
with worries
and there's
little room
for dreams.

Worry
is a waste—
of time,
energy, life.

Worry,
like junk food,
adds unneeded
weight.

Life is a gift.
Open the box
and enjoy.

Worry is a vehicle
that drives you
nowhere
but crazy.

Worries cast
big shadows
over the smallest
of things.

When worries
call, hang up.

Leave your
worries behind.
Go on a
vacation—with
yourself.

The quality of
your thoughts
determines
the quality of
your life.

Two's a crowd
when you hang
out with
a negative
thought.

Retreat from
your cares—
spend an hour
each day doing
what you love.

Change is scary,
true, but so is
having everything
stay the same.

Your future
is shaped in the
present—
one moment,
one thought
at a time.

Sometimes you've got to float before you can get to shore.

Befriend faith
and the world
becomes
a friend.

Worries are
a veil that hides
the beauty of
the world.

Many worries
stop when we
stop waiting for
permission.

When you don't
know what
to do, let your
heart advise.

Why bring old
ways of thinking
to a brand-new
day?

Things change—
and so do you.

Step out
of character
into a
new way of
thinking, doing,
being.

Fears shorten
our days;
actions
lengthen them.

Enough of the
dress rehearsal.
Get on
that stage!

Some forks in the road require that you take both paths.

You'll never know
what's behind
the door if you
don't open it.

The world is rich;
only our
thoughts
are poor.

Life
is not a race
but a leisurely
walk.

Make
the unknown
known.

Don't ask,
"What if?"
Ask,
"What now?"

Don't wring
your hands;
reach out
and touch.

A life
lived fully
has no room
for worry.

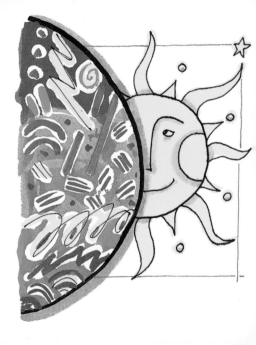

Worries are
an eclipse
that blocks
the sun.

Worry is a
slow leak
that can sink
the sturdiest
of ships.

Worry is a
coward that
disappears
in the face
of facts.

Stop worry
in its tracks—
make a
decision.

Actions
speak louder
than words—
and worries.

If you don't live
in the moment,
where do you
propose to live?

Each day is
a clean slate,
awaiting your
special imprint.

Let go of
what's beyond
your control
and it will
no longer
control you.

Why worry
about the future?
You have
enough to do
in the present.

Worry is static,
making it difficult
for positive
messages to
come through.

Go on a
positive-thinking
diet.

Many an
obstacle
is really a
stepping stone.

Count
every lesson
you learn as
a success.

Go within
to gain strength,
momentum,
perspective.

Follow your own path, your own thoughts, your own heart.

Sometimes
it's good to
shift your focus
from the horizon
to what's close
at hand.

Why wait
for the right
moment?
Make the moment
right,
right now.

Stop,
look,
listen,
breathe.

Life is meant
to be lived
one day
at a time,
not one worry
at a time.

Sweat the small
and big stuff—
work out
to work
through.

Small steps,
giant leaps—
both get you
over the
mountain.

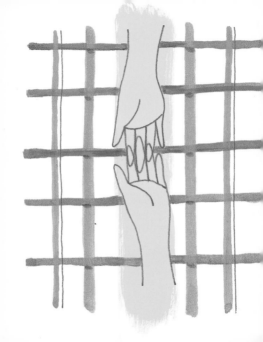

Double-team
your problems;
enlist the
support of
a friend.

Create
a sacred space
within yourself,
where only
peaceful
thoughts
may enter.

If you can't say
anything nice,
don't say
anything at all—
especially if
you're talking
to yourself.

Every road
has its bumps
and curves—
and vistas that
let you see the
big picture.

Why walk,
when you
can soar;
why worry,
when you
can live?

Security
is not
opportunity.

We often fear
what we want
most.

Take up
gardening—
clear, prune,
and weed
worries from
your life.

Do what you think you cannot do and all else becomes possible.

Worry is a luxury
you can't afford.

Expect
the best
and you'll
meet your
expectations.

You need
only one person's
permission—
your own.

Live fully
in the moment
and the moment
lives forever.